COUNTRIES

Spain

Ruth Thomson

Explore the world with **Popcorn** - your complete first non-fiction library.

Look out for more titles in the Popcorn range. All books have the same format of simple text and striking images. Text is carefully matched to the pictures to help readers to identify and understand key vocabulary. www.waylandbooks.co.uk/popcorn

Published in paperback in 2013 by Wayland
Copyright © Wayland 2013

Wayland
Hachette Children's Books
338 Euston Road
London NW1 3BH

Wayland Australia
Level 17/207 Kent Street
Sydney NSW 2000

Produced for Wayland by
White-Thomson Publishing Ltd
www.wtpub.co.uk
+44 (0)843 208 7460

Editor: Steve White-Thomson
Designer: Amy Sparks
Picture researchers: Ruth Thomson/Steve White-Thomson
Series consultant: Kate Ruttle
Design concept: Paul Cherrill

British Library Cataloging in Publication Data
Thomson, Ruth, 1949-
   Spain -- (Countries)(Popcorn)
   1. Spain--Juvenile literature.
   I. Title II. Series
   914.4-dc22

ISBN: 978 0 7502 7199 8

10 9 8 7 6 5 4 3 2

Wayland is a division of Hachette Children's Books,
an Hachette UK company.
www.hachette.co.uk

Printed and bound in China

Picture Credits: Alamy: Barbara Boensch 15; Corbis: David Lefranc/Kipa front cover; Dreamstime: Noam Armonn 11l; Photolibrary: Christophe Boisvieux 19; Shutterstock: Ana del Castillo 1/10, Elena Aliaga 2/8, Jo Chambers 5, Konstantin Shishkin 6, David Hughes 7, dlnicolas 9, Mircea Bezergheanu 11r, Botond Horváth 12, mangojuicy 13b, Tim Tran 13t, Marek Slusarczyk 14, Vinicius Tupinamba 17, Audi Dela Cruz 16tr, Carolina 16mr, Somatuscan 16br, irabel8 16bl, Jonas San Luis 16tl, Matt Trommer 18, Ashiga 20, Bill Florence 21, Dusan Po 22; Neil Thomson 23

Every effort has been made to clear copyright. Should there be any inadvertent omission, please apply to the publisher for rectification.

Contents

Where is Spain?

Here is a map of Spain.

Spain is in southwest Europe.

Bay of Biscay

FRANCE

Bilbao

ANDORRA

P y r e n e e s

River Duoro

River Ebre

Lloret de Mar

Barcelona

PORTUGAL

Madrid

River Tajus

Minorca

Majorca

SPAIN

Valencia

Ibiza

Benidorm

Mediterranean Sea

Seville

Sierra Nevada

Malaga

Cadiz

Marbella   Torremolinos

Atlantic Ocean

EUROPE

MOROCCO

ALGERIA

Madrid is the capital of Spain.
It is in the centre of the country.
The King of Spain has a palace there.

The Royal Palace has 2,800 rooms,
more than any other palace in Europe.

Land and sea

The high Pyrenees mountains in the north are between Spain and France. There are dry plains in the centre of the country and good farmland near the coasts.

In winter, people go skiing and snowboarding in the Pyrenees.

Spain has long coasts. The north coast faces the Atlantic Ocean. The east and south coasts face the Mediterranean Sea.

The north is cool and rainy, so the land is very green.

The weather

Spain is the sunniest country in Europe. In summer, the Mediterranean coast has twelve hours of sunshine every day.

Millions of tourists crowd the beaches. Many stay in big hotels.

In winter, it is freezing cold on the
plains and near the mountains.
There is often heavy snow.

The tops of the Sierra Nevada mountains are
covered with snow for six months of the year.

Town and country

Most Spanish people live in towns or cities. The shopping streets in the city centres are often closed to traffic.

Shops stay open late. In the early evening, people often take a stroll through the streets.

In the country, many Spanish farmers grow oranges, lemons, olives, sunflowers or grapes. These crops ripen in the long, sunny days of summer.

Olive trees can live up to 500 years.

Orange blossom smells very sweet.

Both olive and orange trees are evergreen. They do not drop their leaves in autumn.

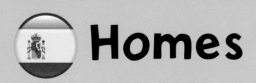

Homes

In towns and cities, many people
live in apartments or houses.
These rarely have gardens,
but often have balconies instead.

The windows have shutters to keep out the hot sun.

In the north, some flats have glassed-in balconies. In the south, houses are white with thick walls and small windows.

The strong glass in these flats in the north protect people from wind and rain.

Houses in the south stay cool in the hot sun.

13

Shopping

People shop for food in supermarkets, indoor markets and small shops.

Busy markets sell meat, fish, fruit, vegetables and cheese.

The Spanish use euros and cents as their money.

There are modern shopping malls in big cities. These are open every day of the week until late at night.

This mall in Barcelona is by the sea. It has an aquarium, as well as lots of shops.

Food

Cooking varies from one area of Spain to another. These are some well-known dishes.

churros (doughnuts) and hot chocolate

empanada (meat or fish pie with onions and peppers)

fabada (beans and pork soup) from the north

gazpacho (cold tomato soup) from the south

paella (rice with seafood and chicken) from Valencia

After work, many people eat hot and cold snacks called tapas with a drink. The Spanish eat dinner very late.

On warm summer nights, people eat and drink at tables outside.

Musicians often play their instruments at open-air cafés.

Sport

Spanish people love their sport. Basketball, tennis, cycling and football are popular.

Real Madrid has won the European Cup nine times, more than any other team.

Spain's national football side is one of the best in the world.

In north-east Spain, people play a
ball game called pelota. Two teams
take turns to hit a rubber ball
against a high wall.

Players wear a glove with a basket on the end.
They catch and throw the ball with it.

Festivals

Every town and village in Spain holds its own festival, called a fiesta. The most important celebrations are in Holy Week before Easter.

Men parade through the streets with holy sculptures on floats.

At festivals in the south, some people dance the flamenco. The dancers click castanets and stamp their feet in time to guitar music.

Female flamenco dancers always wear long frilly dresses and high-heeled shoes.

Speak Spanish!

¡Hola! *(o-la)*	Hello
¿Que tal? *(kay tal)*	How are you?
Vale *(bah-lay)*	OK
¡Adiós! *(ad-yoss)*	Goodbye
Por favor *(por fav-or)*	Please
Gracias *(grath-yass)*	Thank you
Si *(see)*	Yes
No *(no)*	No
Me llamo… *(may ya-mo)*	My name is…

Spain's flag has the Spanish coat of arms on it.

A Spanish ball game

Spanish children call this ball game
'Burro'. This means 'donkey' in Spanish.

1. One player bounces a ball and
hits it against a wall with one hand.

2. The second player must catch
the ball before it bounces.

3. The second player then bounces
the ball and hits it against the wall
for the first player to catch.

4. If you don't catch the ball before
it bounces, you get the letter B (of
Burro). Every time you miss the ball,
you get another letter of 'Burro'.

The first player to complete the
word 'Burro' loses the game.

Glossary

apartment a home with rooms all on the same level of a building

balcony a platform on the outside of a building with railings or a wall around it

capital the city in a country where the government is

castanets two shells made of hard wood, that dancers click together in their hands

market a place with stalls where people buy and sell things

plains large, flat areas of land

tourist someone who travels for fun or on holiday

Index